P.R.A.I.S.E.

—effectively guiding student behavior

P.R.A.I.S.E.
—effectively guiding student behavior

By Dr. Beth Ackerman

purposeful design.
p u b l i c a t i o n s
A Division of ACSI
Colorado Springs, Colorado

Purposeful Design Publications is the publishing division of the Association of Christian Schools International (ACSI) and is committed to the ministry of Christian school education, to enable Christian educators and schools worldwide to effectively prepare students for life. As the publisher of textbooks, trade books, and other educational resources within ACSI, Purposeful Design Publications strives to produce biblically sound materials that reflect Christian scholarship and stewardship and that address the identified needs of Christian schools around the world.

Unless otherwise identified, all Scripture quotations are taken from the Holy Bible, New International Version® (NIV®), © 1973, 1978, 1984 by International Bible Society. All rights reserved worldwide. The "NIV" and "New International Version" are trademarks registered in the United States Patent and Trademark Office by International Bible Society. Use of either trademark requires the permission of International Bible Society.

Other quotations are taken from the New American Standard Bible (NASB), © 1960, 1962, 1963, 1968, 1971, 1972, 1973, 1975, 1977, 1995, 1997 by the Lockman Foundation.

Printed in the United States of America

16 15 14 13 12 11 10 09 08 07   1 2 3 4 5 6 7

Library of Congress Cataloging-in-Publication Data
Ackerman, Beth.
   PRAISE—effectively guiding student behavior / by Beth Ackerman.
      p. cm.
   Includes bibliographical references.
   ISBN 978-1-58331-089-2

   1. Praise. 2. Students--Psychology. 3. Motivation in education. 4. Effective teaching. I. Title.
   LB1065.A235 2007 371.39'3--dc22

                                                                                    2007026714

Catalog #6587

Designer: Chris Tschamler
Editorial team: Gina Brandon, Karen Friesen, Christina Nichols

Purposeful Design Publications
A Division of ACSI
PO Box 65130 • Colorado Springs, CO 80962-5130
Customer Service: (800) 367-0798 • Website: www.acsi.org

To all the youth who have tested and tried my faith—
I praise God for what you taught me.

Introduction

We all, like sheep, have gone astray, each of us has turned to his own way; and the Lord has laid on him the iniquity of us all. (Isaiah 53:6)

Anyone who works in education probably knows that a teacher's greatest challenge in the classroom is behavior management. Although there is a wealth of books on the subject, few such books have been written from a Christian perspective for Christian educators. In addition, many of these books give advice for managing the general population of students, while most of a teacher's stress comes from a few particular students who challenge authority, break rules, and interrupt instruction. Even the most knowledgeable and experienced teachers often find themselves stumped on what to do with these difficult students. This guidebook attempts to address these concerns by going a step further; it not only gives general behavior management advice but also offers tips for handling the challenging student from a Christian perspective, coupled with tried-and-true research.

For some reason, when dealing with their students' behavior, some teachers throw out everything they have ever known about teaching. But the bottom line is that appropriate behavior should be taught. To teach appropriate behavior, teachers must model proper behavior, assess the students' current behavior, and create plans for improved behavior. When a teacher asks a student, "What is four plus four?" and the student's answer is "9," an effective teacher would never respond, "Excuse me! Do you think I am playing? You should go to the principal's office right now for what you just said. I'm going to write your name on the board." Instead, an effective teacher would teach that student the correct answer and show him or her why the original answer was wrong. An effective teacher would help the student complete the problem correctly and help the parents practice completing the problem with the student at home.

The same concept applies to behavior management. Instead of overwhelming teachers by telling them about the abundance of resources on behavior management, this guidebook will show how teachers can respond to their students' behavior challenges by building on what they already know about teaching. To help teachers apply their instructional skills to improving their students' behavior, this book covers the keys to successful classroom management using the acronym PRAISE: being **p**roactive, using **r**einforcements, **a**ssessing and analyzing the **i**ntent of misbehavior, being **s**incere, and **e**mpowering the Holy Spirit in students (Ackerman 2006). This mnemonic tool serves as a primer for evaluating and guiding student behavior and for creating a positive and structured classroom environment. In addition to being a great tool for remembering much of the information covered in this guidebook, PRAISE can be used in an in-service format to prepare fellow educators for dealing with challenging students.

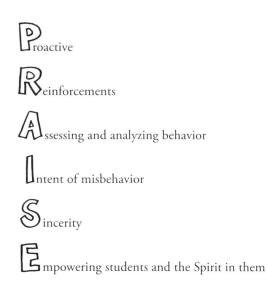

Proactive

Reinforcements

Assessing and analyzing behavior

Intent of misbehavior

Sincerity

Empowering students and the Spirit in them

PRAISE: Proactive

Proactive (the *p* in PRAISE) behavior management is the primary key for preventing negative behaviors. An effective teacher is proactive much more often than reactive. Strong or experienced teachers know they can head off behavior problems by preparing in advance to avoid situations that might encourage these problems. Such proactive preparation involves arranging classrooms appropriately, posting classroom rewards and consequences, and fostering a positive, structured environment (Wong and Wong 2004; Carpenter and McKee-Higgins 1996). A teacher can also take other proactive measures. The sections below more fully describe a proactive teacher.

A Proactive Teacher Is Well Liked

A Proactive Teacher Has Fun

Many students disrupt class and wind up in the principal's office simply because their classroom is not an enjoyable place for them or because they do not clearly understand what the teacher expects from them. Sometimes the problem is a curriculum that either does not challenge students or is not innovative, causing students to become bored. But if teachers use some creativity in lesson planning, they can help students enjoy the classroom and students will prefer to be in class rather than in the principal's office. Providing a variety of activities can aid teachers in making the classroom more enjoyable. At first, teachers may feel that this endeavor takes more time and puts their control of the class at risk, but they will see that sticking with it often results in a more fulfilling work environment—making the classroom more fun and more controlled because the students are engaged in their own learning. Students can sense when a teacher is uncomfortable or unhappy in the classroom, and if the teacher does not want to be there, why should the students? Differentiating instruction and assessment creates a fun environment where the teacher and the students want to be.

A Proactive Teacher Is Positive

Another common reason students misbehave is that they feel threatened in the classroom; they prefer to be in the principal's office where they feel safe because there they won't look foolish in front of their teacher and peers. Since students who feel inadequate tend to act out, the classroom must be an atmosphere where students feel safe and experience success. Positive teachers realize that all human beings, including themselves, fall short of perfection. When coping with a challenging student, positive teachers remember to problem solve for solutions instead of worrying about missteps.

Therefore, while maintaining high standards, positive teachers foster an environment where all students can feel successful. Humor can be a wonderful tool for implementing such grace, for both teachers and students. Teachers who realize their own limitations can laugh at their mistakes and more easily forgive the mistakes of their students. However, when creating a fun atmosphere, it is important for teachers to use humor as a tool, not as a weapon. Particularly when dealing with adolescent students, teachers can sometimes create an environment of ridicule, though they have the better intention of fostering a relaxed and lighthearted atmosphere. Teachers should make sure that students are not the center of jokes, and they should always encourage rather than criticize students.

Does this advice go against the biblical warning about sparing the rod? Not necessarily. Although there is a common belief that students should want to behave and that a teacher's role is to discipline students by catching them when they are out of line, the rod of correction must be put in the context of the biblical description of the good shepherd; the sheep know his voice, and he knows his sheep (John 10:4, 14). The sheep do not want for anything because they lie in green pastures and are beside the still waters (Psalm 23). Just as the sheep would not want to leave the good shepherd's field, a student should not want to leave an effective teacher's classroom. An effective teacher, like the good shepherd, must know his or her sheep and provide for their needs. An effective teacher is a proactive teacher who creates a fun and safe environment for students before resorting to using the rod.

A Proactive Teacher Is Well Respected

In being proactive, it is also important for a teacher to find the balance between being well liked and being well respected. It is common for novice teachers, particularly those teaching the secondary levels, to be concerned about students liking them. They may find that they have befriended the students in order to achieve this goal. While doing so, they may have not gained the necessary respect from the students. But teachers can be proactive in having a classroom that is fun and innovative while still maintaining structure and standards, and thus be liked and respected.

A Proactive Teacher Is Structured

To create a proactive classroom, a teacher must first create a structured classroom. Classroom structure can preempt behavior problems. For example, hyperactive students commonly sit next to a window or near a computer where they can be easily distracted, and students who get along generally sit close together. Another common mistake found in elementary classrooms is that desks are arranged in groups where some students have their backs to the teacher or the center of instruction (for example, the white board or transparency screen). To be fully engaged, students must always face instruction. In creating a structured classroom, it is important to carefully consider the arrangement of the classroom, not only where students sit in relation to other students but also other classroom considerations such as students' proximity to the teacher, location of distractions, and students' view of class instruction (Emmer, Evertson, and Worsham 2003). Time devoted to such forethought can prevent problems, saving time and stress later.

A Proactive Teacher Is Organized

It is important that the students see their teacher as organized, both in modeling proper behavior and in being prepared for instructional time. First, teachers should be held to the same expectations that students are held to. If students are expected to be on time and be prepared with paper, pencils, and correct text, teachers should also begin class on time and have the lessons ready. Such consistent modeling is essential in reinforcing proper behavior. Second, instructional time should be well planned, because most referrals occur during nonstructured academic time. Any principal would probably say that most discipline problems happen during lunchtime, bus rides, physical education, and breaks between classes. Therefore, it is vital that students be engaged in structured activity during every moment they are in class. For students with behavioral problems such as conduct disorders or hyperactivity, it is important that teachers keep to a schedule as much as possible so that the students' school day is predictable. This organization promotes a structured environment, and it is the preventive, proactive way to prevent behavior problems.

A Proactive Teacher Moves Around the Classroom

Teachers who stay behind their desk or at the lecture podium will typically miss opportunities to engage students in learning. To be able to take advantage of any and all teachable moments, teachers must be aware of what their students are doing. The classroom should be arranged in a way that allows for teacher movement and enables teachers to always keep their eyes on the students. A perimeter around the room may need to be created to allow the teacher to walk around. This arrangement provides the added benefit of students' being able to walk about the room without walking between desks. In addition, teachers must watch for possible behavior concerns in their students. It is unfortunate when an incident occurs and a teacher has to tell parents or the principal that he or she did not see what happened. Teachers are entrusted with supervising their students, and challenging students will look for opportunities to act out when their teacher is not looking. Teacher movement can minimize such opportunities, preventing later problems.

A Proactive Teacher Establishes Clear Classroom Rules

Teachers devote much time to planning for the academic calendar and to creating lesson plans, units, and curriculum. They should give the same attention to planning for appropriate behavior in the classroom and the school building. And a well-respected teacher (who teaches any of the age groups—elementary, middle, or high school students) begins by posting clear and concise classroom rules, rewards, and consequences. There should be only four to five rules that emphasize core classroom values, since even six rules become too many and too overwhelming for students to remember. Teachers must use rules to stress nonnegotiable principles. All rules should be stated in a positive manner to encourage a safe and positive atmosphere. The rules should be visible in the classroom, and the students should be taught what each rule means. Teachers should not assume that students have prior knowledge; they must explain the rules at the beginning of the year in order for students to learn what each rule and expectation means, because, for example, some students may not know what it means to stay on task. Once a teacher is sure that his or her students know and understand the rules, those rules can be properly enforced. Below are examples of correct and incorrect rules:

RULES STATED CORRECTLY	RULES STATED INCORRECTLY
Be kind to one another and respect others	Do not talk while the teacher is talking
Submit work in a timely manner	Do not talk without permission
Come to class prepared	No cursing or hitting
Stay on task	Do not come in late
Raise hand when speaking	Do not write notes to other students

A Proactive Teacher Is Consistent

One of the first keys to being consistent is modeling appropriate behavior. As previously noted, if students are expected to be on time, organized, and prepared, then it is important for teachers to *consistently* do so as well. As Scripture notes, students follow not only the instruction of their teacher but the behavior of their teacher as well: "But everyone, after he has been fully trained, will be like his teacher" (Luke 6:40, NASB). Paul, in Philippians 4:9, says, "The things you have learned and received and heard and seen in me, practice these things, and the God of peace will be with you" (NASB). As with instructing any subject, teachers must model appropriate behavior. For example, when teaching algebra, a teacher would model the proper order of operations in solving a problem, reinforcing any verbal instruction that preceded it. So too must consistent modeling of behavior follow any verbal or written instruction on classroom rules. Consistency must also be maintained in rule enforcement. In addition to having clear and concise rules, teachers must enforce these rules in a consistent manner by providing rewards and consequences for breaking these rules. Further ideas for reinforcing rules will be covered in the next section.

A Proactive Teacher Prays for Guidance

Furthermore, the *p* in proactive can also involve prayer. It goes without saying that Christian school teachers need to pray for their students. But they also need to pray for their own ability to reach these students and for patience in finding solutions to reaching these students. Trusting that God will work in the situation is essential for serving difficult students, and because of the importance of this principle, it will be discussed in more detail in the section on Sincerity.

P
R
A
I
S
E

PRAISE: Reinforcements

Reinforcements (the *r* in PRAISE) must be used by the teacher to maintain discipline. Since teachers use reinforcements such as grades in teaching academic concepts, so too can they use reinforcements in teaching students to manage their behavior. These reinforcements can be positive as well as negative. The saying "Spare the rod, spoil the child" applies here. The *r* in PRAISE could be seen as the "rod" of the parable of the good shepherd, as discussed in the previous section. The shepherd does not use only the rod to steer the sheep in the right direction by striking the sheep; he also uses the hook to gently guide the sheep. In addition to the rod, the shepherd also employs many other techniques for guiding the sheep, such as knowing and providing for all of the needs of the sheep, as shown in Psalm 23.

In the same way, teachers can implement many types of positive and negative reinforcements, including eye contact, detention, a pat on the back, or a contingency contract. When deciding on which reinforcement to use, teachers should always try the least restrictive option first and move to a higher level only after attempting to gain control at a low level. For example, before sending a student to the office, a teacher might find that discussing the problem with the student will bring about the desired result. Only when a variety of positive and negative techniques are used in a consistent manner do the "sheep" listen to their teacher's voice (John 10:3).

Teachers should try a variety of reinforcements instead of giving up if the first is unsuccessful. A teacher who is ineffective and reactive rather than proactive might make reactive comments such as the following without addressing the problem: "One more time, and I'm sending you to the office" or "Leave this class." Administrators do not appreciate this approach, and as this type of teacher will find out, it is easier to gain the support of an administrator after exhausting all possible actions in the classroom. Effective teachers employ more positive reinforcements than negative ones. Doing so helps maintain a fun and positive classroom atmosphere where good behavior is rewarded. Most important, good teachers do not fear positive and negative reinforcements; when implemented correctly, these techniques work well.

Reinforcements Must Be Implemented Fairly

As noted above, it is important that teachers be consistent in implementing reinforcements. But there is a difference between fairness and consistency.

P
R
A
I
S
E

Being consistent is recognizing that teachers always give a consequence when a rule is broken. However, teachers may give different consequences for different students, depending on individual student needs. One student may need only a stern look to get back on task, while another student may need a call home. Students may not think this practice is fair, but actually, it is fairer. Just as some students need different types of instruction to the various modalities, students need behavior management techniques that are more appropriate for their individual needs. Assessing the behavior and determining the intent of behavior will guide teachers through making these correct decisions just as they do for learning modalities. This principle will be discussed more fully later in this guidebook.

Reinforcements Must Be Implemented Immediately

In order for rewards and consequences to be effective, they must be given immediately following the infraction. Students need to recognize limits, to know exactly when they have made an error in their behavior. Again, just as in teaching, immediate feedback is always better for improving learning. Although teachers should respond to an inappropriate behavior immediately, they should always remain calm and matter-of-fact when giving a consequence. *There is never a reason for teachers to shout, yell, or talk down to students.* Teachers can be stern without raising their voice, and yelling is inconsistent with the appropriate behavior that teachers are to model for students. In addition, to prevent students from acting out, it is also always better to separate challenging children or adolescents from the group before setting limits for the challenging students. Just as a student who receives an F should be protected from the rest of the class knowing his or her grade, a student who has behavioral challenges should be protected from the ridicule of his or her peers. There is a place for using peer pressure to promote positive behavior, but it is better when used for positive reinforcement rather than negative consequences.

Reinforcements Should Target a Specific Behavior

Having reinforcements that target a specific behavior can be one of the most important steps for giving rewards and consequences. To effectively deal with a challenging student, a specific target behavior needs to be identified. If a broad abstract category or feeling is broken down to a specific behavior, it is possible to respond to it and students can better understand acceptable and unacceptable behavior and take control of their actions. For example, if a student were having trouble with anger, then that student would not be punished for the abstract quality, anger. Rather, the teacher would need to identify a specific behavior such as rolling eyes, cursing, or throwing an item. Just as teachers do when determining the objective of a lesson plan, they must determine the specific, observable behavior that needs to be changed. Identifying a specific behavior aids teachers in communicating with students, parents, and administrators about the behavior that needs work. For example, a teacher may tell Johnny to not be disrespectful, but Johnny may not understand what that even means. The teacher should address a more specific, identifiable behavior of Johnny's, such as rolling his eyes at the teacher. Often, just identifying the problem can help the student change his or her behavior.

Identifying the Problem
(adapted from the Center for Effective Collaboration and Practice 1998)

PROBLEM BEHAVIOR	CONCRETE DEFINITION
Sue is aggressive.	Sue throws her book and other possessions at other students when she is frustrated with work.
Carlos is disrespectful.	Carlos rolls his eyes at authority figures when given commands by them.
John is hyperactive.	John does not sit for more than a few minutes at a time. John does not complete his work. John talks during class at inappropriate times and without permission.

Reinforcements Should Be Implemented in Stages, from Least Restrictive to Most Restrictive

It is always difficult to determine what types of rewards or punishments to use. But it is always important to start with the simplest, least restrictive reinforcement. Doing so teaches the student to internalize the behavior rather than to be motivated by fear of the teacher's severe punishment or be bribed by the teacher's excessive reward. Before suspending a student from school or sending a student to the principal's office, teachers should first try to ignore the behavior, give a stern look, or use proximity to the teacher. Or better yet, teachers should reward the students who are doing what they are supposed to do or "catch" a student who is being good though he or she typically causes problems. Teachers should teach appropriate behavior before using more extreme measures. A teacher would not give a student an F on his or her report card before showing the steps to learning an academic skill. This same concept applies to behavior. In addition, it is best to rely on positive reinforcements more often than negative ones because positive reinforcements more effectively promote appropriate behavior. Most approaches for dealing with student disruptions involve the use of various forms of punishment, and some of these approaches may make a school safer or calmer by removing the offending students. But studies have shown that they have little effect on encouraging students to perform socially appropriate behaviors (Maag 2001). Below are examples of positive and negative reinforcements:

SAMPLE POSITIVE REINFORCEMENTS	SAMPLE NEGATIVE REINFORCEMENTS
Positive words	Verbal reprimands, frowns
Positive calls home	Rule reminders
Behavioral contracts	Loss of privileges in the classroom
Points and levels system	Imposing in-class separation (time-out)
Token economy	Removal from classroom (time-out or isolation room/area)
	Sending home

Many veteran teachers have mastered these techniques. They naturally jump in and out of their behavioral repertoire without breaking a stride in their academic teaching. They use proximity control by standing at the desk of an off-task student, while turning to Johnny and giving him a wink for doing a great job, and then they turn their head to the other side of the room to give a disappointing look to Chris. Sometimes this type of teaching goes unnoticed because these classrooms tend to run smoothly. But teachers who are seeking ways to address behavior concerns in their classrooms would do well to watch these veteran teachers at work. Understanding and using the "least restrictive before the more restrictive" technique also helps a teacher to communicate better with parents and administrators when more assistance is needed. Most administrators greatly appreciate teachers who can manage student behavior within their own classrooms. However, when help is needed from home or from the principal, it is best if the teacher can articulate what has already been tried before needing this assistance.

REINFORCEMENTS FROM LEAST RESTRICTIVE TO MOST RESTRICTIVE

1. Proximity control	7. Rewards
2. Voice control	8. Token economy
3. Pause—stop what you are doing	9. Loss of privileges
	10. Phone calls home
4. Distraction	11. Separation from the group
5. Eye contact	12. Referral to principal
6. Rule reminder	

In addition to these positive and negative reinforcements, some techniques can be very effective tools that can give teachers other options for managing behavior, such as cooperative learning. But sometimes these techniques can be misunderstood or used improperly. The discussion below will provide a primer to aid teachers in considering their options.

Cooperative Learning Groups Can Be Used to Reinforce Appropriate Behavior

Cooperative learning is a wonderful technique that uses peer pressure to reinforce appropriate behavior. In addition to allowing students to work in groups to earn points and prizes, cooperative learning gives the teacher the opportunity to direct attention to positive behavior. But there are keys to making this technique successful. First, teachers should not take points away from the groups. The idea is that the students have already earned these points and taking them away is taking something that the students have already earned. Rather, the teacher can "catch students being good" and give them additional awards. Again, the teacher would not take a grade from a student who has already earned the grade. Second, the teacher must carefully consider the best way to arrange the groups. And as research shows, cooperative learning works best with heterogeneous groups—ones that represent different academic levels and talents (King-Sears 1997).

A Token Economy Can Be Used to Reinforce Appropriate Behavior

A token economy, listed as a sample positive reinforcement, can be used within the cooperative learning technique, but this approach is typically used for individual students for a specific and observable behavior. An example of how this approach can be used is to reward the student who has difficulty staying focused on his or her work with some sort of token during times when he or she is on task. Again, a token cannot be taken away once the student has already earned it. It is important to note that this plan most often fails when teachers give tokens on their own personal whim. The plan then becomes the teacher's behavior management plan rather than the student's plan. In order to be student driven and not teacher driven, the time intervals for receiving the reward are predetermined by the teacher. And a timer should be set to go off at periodic intervals, depending on the data collected during the assessment of the behavior. For example, if according to the data, the student gets off task approximately every fifteen minutes, the timer should be set to go off approximately every fifteen minutes for the reward (Walker, Shea, and Bauer 2004). That way, the student can predict the consequences of his or her actions and thus further assist the student in internalizing the appropriate behavior.

Time-Outs Can Be Used to Discourage Unwanted Behavior

The use of time-outs has been controversial. There are those who feel that time-outs can be humiliating or ineffective. Actually, most teachers use this technique even if they do not call it time-outs. The following are some examples of modified time-outs:

- Sitting out during recess

- Eating lunch separated from friends

- Sitting in the hallway

- Having assignments taken away while sitting quietly

- Sitting outside the principal's office

When used correctively and appropriately, a time-out can be an effective technique. First, as with any technique, there needs to be support for the technique from parents and the administration. This support will ensure consistency and encourage student compliance. Second, expectations for these time-outs should be posted. Since a time-out is to be seen as a negative consequence, these expectations may be stated in the negative, such as no noises, no gestures, no working on class work, or no excessive movements. Third, the teacher should be careful and not assign too much time. Experts say that a student should not sit in time-out for more than one minute for each year of age. A seven-year-old student would not do more than a seven-minute time-out, therefore, a five-minute time-out would be appropriate for this student (Evertson, Emmer, and Worsham 2003).

The Difficult Student

Most teachers already know and use the classroom management techniques discussed up to this point (being **p**roactive and using **r**einforcements), but the importance of these steps cannot be minimized. They are the foundation of any effective behavior management plan. Most students respond well to them, but all too often, these wonderful attempts do not address the student who has behavior problems. The following steps for handling chronic classroom disruptions build on the first two techniques and principles.

PRAISE: Assessing

The first thing a teacher should do to determine how to handle a behavioral challenge is to **a**ssess (the *a* in PRAISE) the situation in which the misbehavior occurs. The first step in assessing the situation is to collect information about the behavior. Answering the following questions provides a place to start: What is the misbehavior? When is it happening? Who is present when the misbehavior takes place? What happened before it occurred? What happens after the misbehavior? To be helpful, the answers to these questions must be specific, not abstract. As mentioned previously, instead of labeling the student's attitude as disrespectful, the teacher should name the specific behavior—the student is rolling his or her eyes. It is much easier to identify, assess, and address a specific behavior than to respond to the abstract emotional quality. There are many tools for assessing these behaviors, from simply counting the number of times a student exhibits a specific behavior in a certain time frame to creating an ABC chart for analyzing behavior: the **a**ntecedent of the behavior, the **b**ehavior, and the **c**onsequence following the behavior (Walker, Shea, and Bauer 2004). This specific information helps teachers identify problem behaviors and develop a plan of action.

A Functional Behavioral Assessment Can Help Teachers Assess Student Behavior

The technical term found in the literature for assessing this behavior is a functional behavioral assessment (FBA). This technique should not be used the first time a student misbehaves; the simpler techniques that were discussed in the previous sections should be tried first. The FBA, on the other hand, is a tool that should be used for a student who has chronic behavioral problems. A sample FBA form is shown on the next page.

(adapted from Miller, Multimodal Functional Behavioral Assessment)

FUNCTIONAL BEHAVIORAL ASSESSMENT

Student Name _____ DOB _____ Date _____

Data Sources: ☐Observation ☐Student Interview ☐Teacher Interview ☐Parent Interview
☐Rating Scales ☐Normative Testing

Description of Behavior:

Setting(s) in Which Behavior Occurs:

Frequency:

Intensity (Consequences of problem behavior on student, peers, and instructional environment):

Duration:

Description of Previous Interventions:

Educational Impact:

Function of Behavior: Specify the hypothesized function for each area checked below.

☐**Affective Regulation/Emotional Reactivity** (identify emotional factors—anxiety, depression, anger, poor self-concept—that play a role in organizing or directing problem behavior):

☐**Cognitive Distortion** (identify distorted thoughts—inaccurate attributions, negative self-statements, erroneous interpretations of events—that play a role in organizing or directing problem behavior):

☐**Reinforcement** (identify environmental triggers and payoffs that play a role in organizing and directing problem behavior):
Antecedents:
Consequences:

☐**Modeling** (identify the degree to which the behavior is copied, whom the behavior is being copied from, and why the behavior is being copied):

☐**Family Issues** (identify family issues that play a part in organizing and directing problem behavior):

☐**Physiological/Constitutional** (identify physiological and/or personality characteristics—developmental disabilities, temperament—that play a part in organizing and directing problem behavior):

☐**Communicating Need** (identify what the student is trying to say through the problem behavior):

☐**Curriculum/Instruction** (identify how instruction, curriculum, or educational environment plays a part in organizing and directing problem behavior):

Collecting Specific Data Helps the Teacher Better Understand Student Misbehavior

Different techniques can be used to aid in collecting information for the FBA. A very simple technique such as the one below helps the teacher tally the number of times a student does a certain identified behavior in any given amount of time. For example, a teacher is having difficulty with a Susie, who speaks out too often without raising her hand. The teacher can quantify the behavior by putting tally marks on a sheet of paper for how many times Susie spoke out during a fifteen-minute period:

Susie ⊀⊦⊦ ⊦⊦⊦ ⊦⊦⊦ ||| *fifteen minutes*

Oftentimes, sharing this information with parents or with older students is all that is needed for them to begin seeing the problem. It is one thing for a teacher to tell a parent that Susie disrupts the class by speaking out, but it is quite another to tell a parent that Susie spoke out of turn thirteen times in a fifteen-minute period. Collecting this information gives the teacher a tool for communicating with others about the problem that is occurring in the classroom. In addition, just as a teacher gives periodic assignments to check a student's progress, a teacher collects this type of data to establish a *baseline* for determining if intervention plans are effective. In order to determine the effectiveness of the plan, the teacher continues to collect data after trying different responses to the student's behavior.

Using an ABC Chart Provides Detailed Information About Student Misbehavior

Using an ABC chart takes the information about student behavior a step further. The chart helps the teacher analyze the intent of the misbehavior as well as the effectiveness of the teacher's response to the behavior. An ABC chart shows the **a**ntecedent (what is taking place before the behavior), the **b**ehavior (the identified misbehavior), and the **c**onsequence (the teacher's response to the behavior). The following chart is an example of an ABC chart to help determine the intent of misbehavior.

P
R
A
I
S
E

ANTECEDENT	BEHAVIOR	CONSEQUENCE
Math lesson/teacher instruction	Spoke out of turn	Ignored student
Homework time (doing math)	Talked without permission	Gave a warning
Reading orally	Asked inappropriate question	Answered the question

Some helpful information can be gathered by using this chart. A teacher can observe in the consequence section that he or she is not responding in a consistent manner and is sending mixed messages to the child. Therefore, before developing an elaborate plan, a teacher may first want to collect data to show that he or she is responding in a consistent manner. When the teacher is being consistent and not sending mixed messages, the antecedent to the behavior can be looked at more closely. In the above example, a pattern emerges. The misbehavior is always occurring during academic time. This is telling since misbehavior happens more typically during unstructured, nonacademic time. One possibility may be that the student is insecure about his or her work and is acting out because of feelings of inadequacy. The next section will cover more details about intent of misbehavior and plans for addressing the reason that students misbehave.

PRAISE: Intent

Identifying the intent (the *i* in PRAISE) of the student's misbehavior is another important key in developing an intervention plan. Like crying toddlers or babies, students communicate through their behavior, and a student who has chronic behavior problems is communicating a need. All too often, the student doesn't know or understand what he or she is attempting to communicate. Students misbehave for many reasons, and it is vital that the teacher understand the reason for the action before reacting.

A classic example of intent of misbehavior can be seen in a student who has learned to receive attention in a negative manner. After determining that the intent of the misbehavior is to receive attention, the teacher should give the student attention for wanted behaviors, while ignoring unwanted ones. Another common problem seen in schools is a power struggle between a teacher and a student. To intervene in this case, a teacher should not be too personally invested in the discipline of this student. Often in this situation, it can be important for the teacher to gain additional support from an administrator or a parent.

Another example of intent of misbehavior can be seen in the ABC chart from the previous section. The behavior occurs during academic time, possibly indicating that the student may be exhibiting feelings of inadequacy. The teacher is responding inconsistently with negative reinforcements rather than treating the feeling of inadequacy by giving the student an opportunity to experience success. In order to react appropriately, the teacher must determine the source and intent of the misbehavior before a specific plan can be developed. There are typically five reasons that challenging students misbehave: testing of limits, attention, power, revenge, and display of inadequacy (Dreikurs, Grunwald, and Pepper 1998).

Students Misbehave When Testing Their Limits

The most common reason that students (or anyone for that matter) do not follow the rules is to test their limits. It is common to continuously test one's limits, as this is the basic human sinful nature. For example, when the speed limit is fifty-five miles an hour, most people will go sixty-two miles an hour in hopes that they will not get pulled over. The same is true in the classroom; students will see how far they can go. A teacher can best know if this is the problem he or she is encountering by whether or not the majority or a large group of students are exhibiting the behavioral problems. These students will take a mile when the teacher gives an inch. The best way for a teacher to combat this issue is to do all the steps from the first two sections, being **p**roactive and using **r**einforcements. The remaining intents of misbehavior, however, may need further planning than what has been discussed thus far.

Students Misbehave When Seeking Attention

A common example of a student seeking attention is the classic class clown. This student wants everyone to pay attention to him or her, using whatever means necessary—humor, aggression, or whatever the case may be. The teacher can recognize the problem by using an ABC chart and seeing that the consequence is always attention. The following are tips for dealing with an attention seeker:

- Ignore misbehavior when possible.

- Give attention for positive behavior when the child is not making a bid for it.

- Realize that reminding, punishing, rewarding, coaxing, and service are undue attention.

Students Misbehave When Seeking Power

Students who are seeking power want to control the classroom or the situation. Sometimes the parents of these students may be in power positions, and they manipulate this control as well. These students struggle for control at any point in their lives, and they believe that power is the way to achieve this control. Someone has to "lose the game." Therefore, the best advice for teachers who are dealing with such students is to just not play the student's game. The following are tips for dealing with a student who is seeking power:

- Withdraw from conflict—do not back down on consequences. Rather, recognize that someone else can help carry through these consequences.

- Help the child to see how to use power constructively. Appeal to the child for help.

- Realize that fighting or giving in only increases the child's desire for power.

- Give options for consequences.

- Set a time limit for making a decision.

Particularly when approaching adolescent students, a teacher can more quickly end a power struggle by setting up a situation in which the student can feel some control while still achieving the teacher's desired result. The teacher can simply give options and set a time limit. For example, a teacher could say softly to the student, to avoid humiliating him in front of his peers, "Johnny, you have five minutes to … (stop what you're doing, go to the principal's office …), or I will have to … (call your parents this afternoon, talk to the coach, get the principal ...)." Learning to state the consequence in this manner is a powerful tool to use with a student who initiates power struggles. It creates a win-win situation rather than a win-lose situation.

Students Misbehave When Seeking Revenge

Determining the intent of behavior in students who are challenging is difficult because they may jump in and out of any of these roles, often because the teacher could have handled the situation better. Below is an all-too-familiar example of how these negative behaviors progress:

Seeking *attention*, Susie is loudly tapping her pencil on her desk. Rather than ignoring this negative, attention-seeking behavior, the teacher, Ms. Smith, commands, "Susie, stop tapping your pencil." Susie, who feels cornered and wants to regain *power* and attention, says, "Make me." The teacher is frustrated and wants Susie to "lose" in a sense, instead of wanting a win-win situation. Therefore, the teacher gets in Susie's face, points a finger, and says, "I'll make you. Go to the principal's office. I'm giving you a 0 on today's work, and I'm going to talk to your mother, young lady." In order to not lose, Susie now wants *revenge* for what the teacher did, and she retaliates with some type of insulting behavior such as saying, "Ms. Smith, your breath stinks."

Sometimes, too, the revenge comes later: the student may have a bad attitude after returning from detention or suspension or after receiving report cards. The following are tips for dealing with a student who is seeking revenge:

- Avoid feeling hurt.

- Avoid punishment, since it is seen as retaliation.

- Build a trusting relationship.

- Find a common interest with this student.

- Convince the child that he or she is loved.

P
R
A
I
S
E

Often, a teacher can just talk to students about these conflicts and let them know they are valued. If consequences must be given to a student who is seeking revenge, the teacher should see if someone else could assist in the consequence. It is often helpful to give a tough love speech to this type of student: "It would be easy for me to ignore what you do. But because I care so much about you and your future, I need to teach you not to respond in this manner."

Students Misbehave to Display an Inadequacy

Some students misbehave to display an inadequacy. Examples include the student who makes holes with an eraser in his or her math book, the student who grunts and pouts in frustration while doing work, and the student who tears up papers and throws them away. These students do not feel adequate. Children living with learning deficits can be helped when teachers and counselors create learning environments that build confidence and encourage accomplishment (Barrett-Kruse, Martinez, and Carll 1998). The following are tips for dealing with a student who displays inadequacy:

- Stop all criticism.

- Encourage any positive attempt, no matter how small.

- Focus on assets.

- Don't be hooked into showing pity, and don't give up. Remember that pity just confirms that they have something to feel sorry for themselves about, and it can teach "learned helplessness."

- Differentiate instruction (King-Sears 1997).

Finding a Web of Support Can Help Teachers Help Their Students

Often, once the intent of behavior is determined, it is necessary for teachers to seek assistance in carrying out a plan of action or determining a behavior intervention plan. A teacher will often look to the parents and the principal for such assistance, but sometimes it can be found in someone else whom the student values and respects, such as a coach, a choir director, a pastor, grandparents, older siblings, peers, church members, other teachers, cafeteria workers, or bus drivers. It is important for a teacher to utilize the available resources to reach a student. Sometimes outside help and attention are needed to carry out consequences or to provide positive attention outside the classroom. A teacher who gets to know his or her students will recognize where assistance can be found and will be creative in utilizing the help of others.

PRAISE: Sincerity

In dealing with any behavioral challenges, it is critical for teachers to approach students with all **s**incerity (the *s* in PRAISE) by seeking what is best for the individual child. Teachers and administrators must demonstrate Christ's love and forgiveness. Students must always feel that their teacher wants what is best for them. Too often, teachers get too personally involved in a difficult situation and forget to always act in their student's best interest, or they become more concerned with their own immediate need of gaining control. In difficult situations, teachers can find themselves in win-lose battles in which the student is punished or in which the teacher feels wronged, rather than in win-win situations in which both the student and the teacher achieve their desired results. Win-win situations also help teachers to become well liked by students. Any successful behavior management plan requires compassion for the needs and the esteem of the students.

The Challenging Student Is Like the Lost Sheep

"Suppose one of you has a hundred sheep and loses one of them. Does he not leave the ninety-nine in the open country and go after the lost sheep until he finds it? And when he finds it, he joyfully puts it on his shoulders and goes home. Then he calls his friends and neighbors together and says, 'Rejoice with me; I have found my lost sheep.' I tell you that in the same way there will be more rejoicing in heaven over one sinner who repents than over ninety-nine righteous persons who do not need to repent." (Luke 15:4–7)

Objections to working with challenging students are commonly heard from teachers and administrators: "We have 350 other students in the building who need our attention," or "I have 24 other students in this class. It isn't fair for this 1 student to take too much of my time." The parable of the lost sheep answers this concern all too clearly: "Does he not leave the ninety-nine in the open country and go after the lost sheep until he finds it?" Of course, there are initial fears that go with this idea. How far should we go? How do we seek to reach the difficult student while nurturing and educating those who have not strayed? But, it is important to see Christ's mission in going after the most challenging and lost people, as shown throughout the Bible, from Jonah to Zacchaeus to Paul.

The Great Commission Calls Christian Teachers to Reach Difficult Students

> He said to them, "Go into all the world and preach the good news to all creation." (Mark 16:15)

> "I was sick and you looked after me, I was in prison and you came to visit me." (Matthew 25:36)

Christian school teachers are able to meet the needs of individual students who have behavior challenges only if the teachers are open to receiving *all* of God's children. The Gospels call for all Christians to reach all people and to set prisoners free. The first tool to assist teachers in making the decision could not be more obvious or overstated—prayer.

Christian Teachers Should Pray for Themselves and for Their Students

Even teachers are human and broken, and it is common for teachers to make mistakes in how they handle challenging students. Prayer and guidance from God can help keep them on track. There are times when teachers feel verbally and physically abused by students and prayer becomes a necessity. There is no exact science in dealing with human behavior, but for seeking success for students, the power of faith and prayer cannot be contended with. On rough days of dealing with challenging behaviors, it is easy for teachers to feel bitter, vengeful, and doubtful of any success for these students. In prayer, however, teachers can welcome the fruit of the Spirit to fill their heart—in order to show love, joy, peace, patience, kindness, goodness, faithfulness, gentleness, and self-control in dealing with these students (Galatians 5:22–23). Other verses that teachers can use for prayer include 1 Thessalonians 5:14, "We urge you, brothers, warn those who are idle, encourage the timid, help the weak, be patient with everyone."

In the busyness of life and teaching, it is easy to just go through the motions of a spiritual life, to say a quick prayer and move on to the next thing on the checklist. To help these students, a teacher must take some time to go deeper into prayer. Richard Foster, in *Celebration of Discipline*, gives a guide for a deeper prayer life. He explains, "Learning to pray for others is to listen for guidance" (1998, 39). He also says, "Imagination often opens the door to faith" (41). Therefore, when teachers pray for their students, they need to imagine the student behaving and being whole. Any teacher who is dealing with a challenging student should spend some time in a prayer study. Books

P
R
A
I
S
E

such as Foster's give advice for praying against evil and for healing prayer that would help both students and teachers through their spiritual journeys.

The challenge of dealing with these students and praying for them also does something for the teacher. It teaches patience and provides an opportunity to show God's love and grace. In addition to praying for Christ to begin working in the hearts of students, a teacher is asking God to work in his or her heart as well. These challenging students challenge teachers. James 1:12 states, "Blessed is the man who perseveres under trial, because when he has stood the test, he will receive the crown of life that God has promised to those who love him." The job of a Christian is not supposed to be easy. When a Christian teacher is being tested and refined, it should be seen as a blessing from the Spirit, who teaches how to better cultivate the fruit of the Spirit.

PRAISE: Empowering

It is most important for teachers to **e**mpower (the *e* in PRAISE) students to manage their own behavior. Galatians 5:22–23 states, "But the fruit of the spirit is … self-control. Against such things there is no law." Ideally, students should be able to manage their own behavior rather than be controlled by outside influences. Empowering students to manage their own behavior can be one of the teacher's greatest challenges. If a teacher asks a student who has a behavior issue to act in a way that seems normal to the teacher, the teacher should remember that the student is learning to behave in a manner that is actually abnormal to the student. However, schools can assist students in this struggle by teaching them with a behavior management plan that students are involved in creating. The goal of such a behavior management plan is for the student to learn how to demonstrate the appropriate behavior without assistance. Schools could allow students to give their own reinforcements and could encourage independent control of behavioral issues.

A Behavioral Contract Can Empower Students

A behavioral contract is an important technique for teaching a child to gain control of his or her own behavior. For example, a child has had his or her name written on the board many times. The parents now expect the call from the teacher or the principal about their child's negative behavior. And the principal is never surprised to find the child waiting outside his or her office. Everything has been tried, and nothing seems to work. This is often because the plan to change the behavior was the teacher's plan. But after analyzing a functional behavioral assessment and determining the student's likes and dislikes, it is often necessary to write a behavior intervention plan, or more simply, a behavioral contract. This contract becomes the student's plan, not the teacher's plan. And the student becomes more responsible for his or her behavior.

This contract is between the student and the teacher, and often between the parents and the administrator as well. It may also involve someone from the student's web of support, such as a coach or a pastor. The contract simply states what will happen if the student exhibits correct behavior and what will happen if the student exhibits negative behavior. An example of the framework for the contract is on the following page.

BEHAVIORAL CONTRACT

If I _____, then I will be able to

_____. If I _____,

then I will need to _____.

_____   _____
Teacher's Signature   Administrator's Signature

_____   _____
Student's Signature   Parent's Signature

This contract should always be available and should always be in the child's sight line, such as on his or her desk or in his or her assignment book. The teacher should remember that the contract must have a specific identified target and must be measurable and observable in order for the student to receive the proper praise and consequences. For example, if Johnny does not interrupt class for twenty minutes, he will be given a check mark. After fifteen check marks, Johnny may choose an assignment that he does not have to complete. If Johnny does not receive any check marks during the class period, then Johnny will lose the privilege of playing video games at home for that evening. Many creative plans and contracts can be implemented to help the student achieve success. It is important for the teacher to use the data collected in the FBA to make sure that the student is not being set up to fail. If the student interrupted class every two minutes while the data was being collected, then twenty minutes may be too long.

Also, the teacher must be sure that the rewards and consequences are ones that matter to the student. To take it to a more meaningful level, the rewards and consequences can match the student's intent of behavior. For example, if a student is seeking attention, the reward can be time with the teacher or peers (depending on the source the student is seeking attention from), and the consequence for negative behavior can be time spent alone. This same concept applies for power. The student can be allowed to lead a discussion or lose the opportunity to be a line leader.

It is also important for challenging and difficult students to focus on only one target behavior. Limiting the focus can be a challenge since there are often many things that teachers would like to change in students, but students can be overwhelmed and feel as if they are being set up to fail if they are given too much to cope with at once. For that reason, a behavioral contract should focus on one identifiable behavior, as previously discussed. Other behaviors can be added as improvements in the first area are made.

Self-Monitoring Empowers Students

Another step in this process is allowing students to keep track of their own successes and failures. This may not be possible at the beginning of a plan. But as a student progresses, the teacher should allow the student to collect and chart his or her own behavioral data. Once again, this is what a teacher would do when teaching an academic subject. Often, teachers have students grade their own work in order to see errors and successes right away. Self-monitoring behavior follows the same principle. The teacher could tape an index card to the corner of the student's desk and the student could put check marks next to negative or positive behaviors at given intervals or when the behavior occurs. For example, the student could put a check mark every time he or she says something polite. Or, as in the behavioral contract example above, the student could put a check mark for every twenty minutes that he or she does not interrupt the teacher. The student could even set a timer or a watch to monitor this time. It is always best to have students record their positive behavior. But self-monitoring can also be used to show students how they are acting in a negative manner, particularly when collecting the beginning data, or to show students how acute a problem is. For example, the teacher can have students learn what disrespect is, and how they are demonstrating disrespect, by asking the students to place a check mark by a behavior whenever they do it or feel like doing it in a specific time indicated. See the example below:

DISRESPECTFUL BEHAVIOR	
Time started: _____ Time ended: _____	
BEHAVIOR	PLACE A CHECK MARK
Rolled eyes	
Talked back to the teacher	
Made fun of or laughed at the teacher	
Didn't make eye contact when addressed	

Spiritual Discipline Empowers Students

Christian schools have an awesome opportunity to address the heart of the matter when dealing with children who have chronic behavior problems. So often, these children have not been taught how to display empathy and regret. They can be given spiritual guidance and tools to assist them in controlling their own behavior. Specifically, the disciplines of prayer, confession, and repentance can be critical for teaching them the fruit of the Spirit. Schools should guide students through study of these areas in order to empower the Spirit to work in the heart of these students.

Being **p**roactive, using **r**einforcements, **a**ssessing and analyzing the **i**ntent of misbehavior, being **s**incere, and **e**mpowering students and the Spirit in them are keys to any successful behavior plan. Using the components in the acronym PRAISE is a simple way to plan, organize, and evaluate successful behavior management.

P
R
A
I
S
E

REFERENCES

Ackerman, Beth. 2006. PRAISE for students with behavioral challenges. *Kappa Delta Pi Record* 43, no. 1:39–41.

Barrett-Kruse, Cathie, Eugene Martinez, and Nanci Carll. 1998. Beyond reporting suspected abuse: Positively influencing the development of the student within the classroom. Special issue. *Professional School Counseling* 1, no. 3:57–60.

Carpenter, Stephanie L., and Elizabeth McKee-Higgins. 1996. Behavior management in inclusive classrooms. *Remedial and Special Education* 17, no. 4:195–204.

Center for Effective Collaboration and Practice. 1998. Addressing student problem behavior. http://cecp.air.org/fba/problembehavior/funcanal.pdf.

Dreikurs, Rudolf, Bernice Bronia Grunwald, and Floy Childers Pepper. 1998. *Maintaining sanity in the classroom: Classroom management techniques.* 2nd ed. Philadelphia, PA: Accelerated Development.

Emmer, Edmund T., Carolyn M. Evertson, and Murray E. Worsham. 2003. *Classroom management for secondary teachers.* 6th ed. Boston: Allyn and Bacon.

Evertson, Carolyn M., Edmund T. Emmer, and Murray E. Worsham. 2003. *Classroom management for elementary teachers.* 6th ed. Boston: Allyn and Bacon.

Foster, Richard J. 1998. *Celebration of discipline: The path to spiritual growth.* 3rd ed. San Francisco: HarperCollins.

King-Sears, Margaret E. 1997. Best academic practices for inclusive classrooms. *Focus on Exceptional Children* 29, no. 7:1–23.

Maag, John W. 2001. Rewarded by punishment: Reflections on the disuse of positive reinforcement in schools. *Exceptional Children* 67, no. 2:173–86.

Miller, Jeffrey A. Multimodal Functional Behavioral Assessment. http://mfba.net/.

Walker, James E., Thomas M. Shea, and Anne M. Bauer. 2004. *Behavior management: A practical approach for educators.* 8th ed. Upper Saddle River, NJ: Pearson Prentice Hall.

Wong, Harry K., and Rosemary T. Wong. 2004. *How to be an effective teacher: The first days of school.* Mountain View, CA: Harry K. Wong Publications.